Sister Wendy's
Story of
Christmas

Prestel

The Story of Christmas is about the birth of a baby. Usually when there is a birth, and especially a birth as important as this, there are four people present. There are the mother and the father. There is a helper, like a doctor or a nurse or a midwife. And there is the baby itself.

This birth took place on or around December 25th, which we now celebrate as Christmas Day, and the name of the mother was Mary. The father was called Joseph. We do not know the name of the helper. But the baby, of course, was Jesus.

No painter was there to see the birth, so artists have always had to paint how they imagine this event to have been. They all stress different things and, therefore, paintings can help us understand the story better, and maybe inspire our own imagination.

There are many things about this birth that may seem strange to us today. One of them is that Jesus was not born in a hospital or even in his own home: he was born in a stable, where an ox and an ass were kept, and his mother had to use straw to fill his cradle. Artists did not know what the stable looked like, but they must have enjoyed themselves painting how they thought it might have looked.

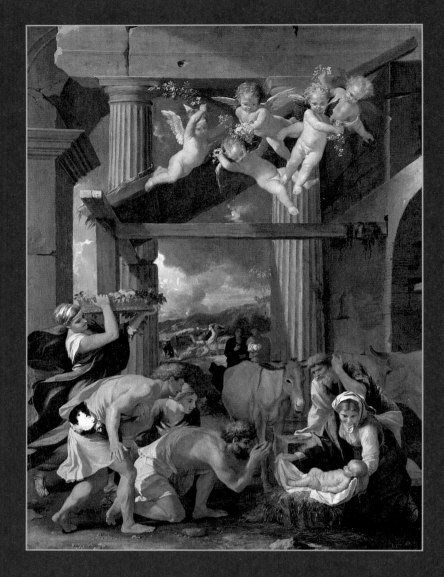

Mother Mary is by far the most important grown-up person in the picture. The great artist Nicolas Poussin (1593–1665) sees her as a most beautiful and gracious lady. Her lovely brown hair gleams in the sunlight, although there are darkening clouds outside. Her dress is painted in the palest pink and deep blue, and she looks at the little Jesus with a half-smile of tender love. She holds him gently as she lays him on the rough straw, amazed at his presence, and quite unaware of anybody else. She is so calm and beautiful that Poussin cannot imagine her in a dirty stable, so he has made a stable out of the kind of ruined temple he could see around him in Rome, which is where Poussin lived. Joseph, the visiting shepherds, and even the animals are all portrayed with the same peaceful dignity and share Mary's joy.

W e do not know the name of the artist that painted this small picture in a Book of Hours (14th century). A Book of Hours is an illustrated prayerbook that people used in the Middle Ages. This painter is not so interested in how beautiful Mary is, but in the way she looks after her baby. She is clutching him to her breast, and feeding him with her milk. She hugs him tightly; she will not let anyone do anything unkind to Jesus while she is there. She is all alone except for Joseph, who has fallen fast asleep. But Mary can find no rest — she is not going to go to sleep — she wants only to kiss her baby and care for him. There is not even a roof over her head in this picture. She is out of doors, as we can see from the tree and the rocks, and she cannot be comfortable lying on the ground, with only her blue cloak to cover her. The ox and the ass are excited, so much so that they seem to be talking to each other. They are trying to understand why Jesus is special, just as today we are trying to do the same. In the picture we saw before, the Holy Family did not have haloes of light around their heads, but here the haloes are very bright. The artist has painted the scene in a complex frame to make us look at it with respect and care.

acopo di Cione (active 1365–1398) — you can tell from his name that he was Italian — is mainly interested in showing how Mary and Jesus are aware of each other right from the start. Jesus is too young to be able to talk, so he looks up at his mother, and she looks back at him in response. Jacopo does not paint Joseph, but surrounds Mary with angels for companions. They add more bright colours to the composition, and one of them is playing music to celebrate the birth. Mary does not even see them. All her attention is fixed on Jesus. She may be cold, as it is a December night, but here she has wrapped the rich red blanket around her child. She does not seem to notice that she is cold and tired, or that she has nowhere to sleep. She simply holds her hands folded in prayer and looks into the eyes of Jesus, while the ox and ass observe it all with amazement. Mary's love and all the glowing colours make this a warm picture, and a very tender one, too.

*A*lbert Herbert (*b.* 1922) is a modern painter and an Englishman. He does not paint what actually took place at the birth of Christ, but what he thinks this birth means. Mary is important because she brought Jesus into the world as a gift from God for anyone who reaches out to him. A little man holds out his arms to receive the baby, and Mary carries him across to let the man hold him. Herbert paints a strange landscape, with no scenery except for a dark hill and a white sky. There could be angels hidden in that sky, or perhaps there is only snow. This is 'our' Christmas, because Jesus is born in our hearts every year, if we ourselves are ready. Behind Mary is a burning bush, referring to a story from the Bible that took place ages before the first Christmas, when God spoke to Moses in the form of a burning bush. So the bush you can see in the picture means that God is still speaking to us, but now he is speaking through Jesus.

*S*ometimes Joseph is not shown in the picture, but he is also an important figure. Mary and Jesus both need him too. He is Jesus' foster father, chosen by God to look after this special child, and Mary also loved him like a father. In this picture, the artist suggests this by painting a very old Joseph, who could even have been Mary's grandfather by the looks of him. Fra Filippo Lippi (*c.* 1406–1469) thinks that poor old Joseph was so exhausted by all that had happened that he simply went to sleep. But he shows Joseph resting without lying down, so that, if any danger should arise, he could take his cane and protect his family. He has made sure that Mary and Jesus are in the warmest part of the stable, close to the animals where it is less uncomfortable. Mary is lost in prayer and has wrapped her long cloak around Jesus to keep him warmer still. It is not a very good situation for a newborn baby and its mother, but Joseph can rest peacefully because he trusts God.

8

Phillipe de Champaigne (1602–1674) — a Frenchman — imagines Joseph to be a much younger man, closer to Mary's age, although we can see that he is going a little bald on top. The shepherds have come to see the baby and have brought their sheep and what looks like a very inquisitive dog. Mary seems a little apprehensive; perhaps she is afraid that the dog might jump up on the manger where the baby is lying. But it is Joseph who is in control. He points the baby out to these unexpected visitors and we can see that he is talking, explaining the wonder of the birth. He may even be telling the dog to keep a respectful distance, as babies are easily frightened. He is standing at the side of the picture, because Joseph is a deeply humble man and never puts himself in the centre. From the side lines he is directing events and seeing that all goes smoothly. His rich, yellow cloak catches the light from the angels, which nobody can see, although the angels can see the people. Their brightness echoes the brightness of the baby Jesus.

An unknown 17th century Italian artist had a soft spot for Joseph, whom he imagines as a handsome young man with dark skin. This artist understands how confusing it must all have been for Joseph. God had told him the secret about Jesus in a dream, but now that it is actually happening, Joseph must be wondering if he is doing all that God expects of the man chosen to be Jesus' foster father. In this scene the shepherds are crowding in with presents. One of them, at the side, is playing the flute, and a boy in front has a whole basket of buns, while he stretches out his arm, offering Mary a chicken. Mary looks up with a rather grim expression. It is just as well that she cannot see the girl coming into the stable with another basket, this time full of live pigeons! It is all getting a bit much. But Joseph remains unfazed, just leaning on his cane. He has a faint halo around his head to show us that he is a truly holy man. God has picked the right person to look after Jesus. Joseph, of course, does not know about the halo. He is in deep thought, gazing at the radiant little Jesus with his fair curls and delicately coloured clothes. Joseph is waiting for God to show him what needs to be done next.

People sometimes say that men prefer to leave all the housework and babycare to women, but in this picture by Master Konrad von Soest (*c.* 1370 – after 1422), painted on the wall of a church about 600 years ago, we can see Joseph preparing supper for his family and sense his great energy. Master Konrad imagines him as an old man, so his eagerness to help with the chores is all the more impressive. He is down on his hands and knees, blowing at the fire, since there is not even a stove in this tumbledown stable. There is also a hole in the roof, which will make it harder to keep the fire going.

Mary has a secret little smile as she cuddles her baby. Perhaps she knows that Joseph is not a very good cook, but she is not going to let on that she can see his difficulties. She and Jesus are both getting ready to be astonished and delighted, whatever their supper tastes like. That is what we do when we love people: we always want to make them happy. Jesus, Mary and Joseph were a totally loving family.

We do not know anything about a human being that helped Mary have her baby, but she did have a helper. God was her helper. Jesus was God's son in a way no other person has ever been, and God made sure that all went well for mother and child when the time came for Mary to give birth. Jesus was born under dreadful circumstances, in just a stable, without even a bed, or a stove to make a hot drink, but God made it all seem easy. Lorenzo Monaco (c. 1370 – 1426) shows the bleakness of the setting, with the little stable just a sort of lean-to perched on dangerous rocks. But everywhere there is dazzling light. Mary is outlined in a gentle glitter, while Joseph raises his head to see where all the glory is coming from. Behind Mary's head we can just make out a mysterious brightness. Of course, we cannot see God, so Lorenzo Monaco, who was a monk — and that is what his surname means — could not paint God. But all that strange and unearthly light makes us very aware, like it makes Joseph aware, that God is present, helping. The animals look surprised, so they also may be conscious of a Divine Presence, and prick their ears in anticipation.

Master Francke (*c.* 1385 – 1436) lived at the same time as Lorenzo Monaco, but has a very different style of painting. He is absolutely determined to make us actually see for ourselves that God is Mary's helper. But since he is not as skilful at using light as Lorenzo, he dares to make an attempt at painting God. He makes it clear that he is not being realistic, though. The sky is coloured an unnatural red and he opens it up to reveal a gentle, bearded old man who is sending rays down to earth. The baby must have travelled on those rays, because it looks as though he has just landed with a bump at his mother's feet! Mary is all alight at this marvellous surprise. She did not see how Jesus arrived, but she is radiant with joy that he has finally come to earth. Before anyone in the painting can see God, the skies will close again. Master Francke wants us to know that, hidden away in mystery, God is always there, loving us, helping us, happy if we are happy.

Some people could not bear the thought that poor Mary had nobody to help her, so they made up a story. In this story, there were two nurses in Bethlehem — the town where the stable was — and these two women were midwives, who help mothers at the birth. One came when she heard Joseph's cry, and saw the whole stable filled with light when Jesus came into the world. She ran to tell the other midwife, Salome, who did not hide her disbelief. Immediately, Salome's hand withered. It was only cured when she came and touched the baby in faith. God does not act so cruelly, withering somebody's hand because they do not believe, but some artists liked the drama of the story. The Salzburger Master (c. 1400) paints a very striking scene. Joseph is exhausted, but he keeps his eye on the goings on. Mary, in dazzling blue robes, contrasts with the red of Joseph's clothes. The artist's intense use of colour shows us how well he can tell such stories. Mary is graciously handing Jesus to the first midwife so that he can be bathed, while Salome is testing the water and feeling somewhat sulky. The painter clearly shows her arms and hand.

At the time the Salzburger Master was painting, everyone would have known this story and what would happen next. Everyone in the scene seems content, except for poor Salome, the woman who does not believe. Even the animals are happy, and the birds on the rafters are spreading their wings and singing. Jesus looks as though he is sorry for Salome, but we know that he will soon be able to help her.

*G*entile da Fabriano (c. 1370 – 1427) shows the next stage of the scene. Salome's hand has crumpled into a stump. Her fellow midwife is sound asleep, but Salome knows that something mysterious and holy is happening, although she has been too stubborn to admit it. She is just about to get up and go across the stable to touch Jesus, and her hand will be put right again. Everything in this picture is painted in bright colours — even the small tree beside Joseph which is beginning to blossom although it is winter. But Salome is wearing a dark cloak to suggest her dark heart, because she has been saying "No" to God: "No, I will not believe." We feel sorry for her and wish Gentile had painted the rest of the story, where Salome moves into that central brightness and lets God heal her hand and her heart. The twisted hand represents her twisted heart, and, just by his touch, Jesus is going to heal both.

16

*J*esus is the only reason for Christmas. He is the star, and Mary and Joseph are the supporting characters. About 800 years ago, an unknown Spanish artist painted this marvellous scene. Joseph is utterly bewildered, and Mary does not quite understand what has happened. Even the ox and ass' eyes are popping out. The only one in this painting who is not in a state of shock is Jesus himself. The artist cannot bear to show him as a tiny and helpless baby. He somehow feels that if Jesus is God, he must have always known what he was doing, even as a baby. Here, the face of the newborn Jesus is alive with intelligence and humour, smiling up at his invisible Father in heaven. He and Mary have haloes of extraordinary shapes, not normal round ones like Joseph. No, these two are very special, and the artist tries to show this through their haloes. Even the crib is not really a manger, but an elaborate casket, and Jesus is wrapped in a green blanket with red swirls. Perhaps this artist is not very accomplished by later standards, but what an amazing painting he has made. The decorations extend even to the cheeks: every face has two large red blobs of colour. Wherever he can, he has added squiggles and decorations to express a sense of festivity. The painting comes straight from his heart.

$\mathcal{P}$aolo de Matteis (1662–
1728) lived nearer to our time — three centuries ago
— but he, too, sees Jesus as fully conscious from the
start. He is much more sophisticated than the
previous painter, but there is no getting away from it:
this is not how a newborn baby behaves. All the same,
this is what this newborn baby has come to tell us:
that we are loved. The little Jesus, radiating light,
opens his arms in love to all the people pushing
around him. He does not only love Mary and Joseph
who are holy, but also stretches out to the ordinary
people, like the plain-looking shepherds. The ox at
his feet has big horns, but he does not feel at all
threatened. When Jesus grows up, he will be put to
death, but he will still reach out to everybody with
love. So, although de Matteis is not painting what
really happened, we get a sense that it did happen
just like this in Jesus' heart. Look at how amazed
Joseph is, and how silently Mary looks on. Even they
are learning about love from Jesus.

Andrea Mantegna (1431–1506) is one of the very great painters. Here, he does not paint the entire scene in the stable; he only paints Jesus in his mother's arms. He shows us a real baby, tired and sleepy. Jesus has been wrapped in swaddling bands, which are strips of cloth wound around a baby to make a neat little parcel, so that the baby cannot kick or move freely. Only Jesus' little hands are showing, free of the bands, but he cannot raise them. So the Son of God has given up all his freedom, as in one way or another all babies do. Mary caresses him thoughtfully, almost sadly. She may be thinking of what will happen in thirty years time, when she will hold her grown-up son in the same way, and he will be wrapped in the linen bands of death. To Mantegna, mother and son look rather alike, with the same red-brown hair and delicate nose and beautiful mouth. And just as Jesus is helpless because of his bands, Mary is helpless, too. She is enclosed in her cape, and all her attention is fixed on Jesus. When we love, we are also con-strained by that love. We are not free to do what we want, or rather, we only want to do what is best for the ones we love. Jesus never laid aside the bands of his love for us, and Mary never laid aside the bands of her love for Jesus.

*G*eorges de la Tour (1593–1652) also shows us these bands. This little Jesus is all alone, there in the centre. Even his mother, in her loose, brightly coloured robe, seems too much in awe to come close to him. Jesus is surrounded by a ring of silent faces, some smiling, some awed, with only the lamb really coming close to him. Has the woman brought water to wash the baby? Or is it soup for Mary? The child has enraptured them all: the woman stands there motionless while the people watch. Babies do nothing except for normal baby things: not very interesting, one would think. But this baby is like no other. Even to be there while he sleeps is a great privilege. Although Joseph is holding a candle and shielding it from the draughts in that windy stable, the real light is coming from little Jesus. He is radiating peace.

21

That night, the skies blazed with light, and angels were heard singing and praising God. The people the angels sang to were the shepherds, who were poor men who had to stay in the fields at night to guard their sheep from wild animals. This artist, painting in a prayer book for the famous Duc de Berry (1340–1416), feels that all those shepherds and great choirs of angels are too much for him. He paints only one of each, a shepherd and an angel, but he paints them so well that we can imagine the story and how amazing it must have been. The poor, astonished shepherd is nearly falling over backwards. His sheep are less excited. The sheep on the left have definitely grasped that something out of the ordinary is occuring, but the rest of the sheep are either uninterested or taken aback. They cannot make out where the sing-ing is coming from. The dog knows, though; he is a very intelligent dog with a fierce jaw to fight off attacking wolves and protect the sheep. Maybe the wolves in hiding can also hear music. The one angel we see is not actually singing, but he is holding a scroll that says that he is bringing tidings of great news — wonderful news, that will change the whole world. The shepherd's hat almost falls off as he strains to hear what this news is. The news is that God has sent his son into the world, and that the shepherd can go and see for himself, if he is quick enough. Even the trees look excited. But until the shepherds reach the stable, no one will know whether they have been dreaming or whether it is all true. We, of course, already know: the angels were speaking the wonder-ful truth!

$\mathcal{R}$embrandt van Rijn (1606–1669) is more interested in showing what it was like in that dim and smoky stable. He realizes that the only light must have come from the glow of the fire and from the lantern; which meant that nobody could see very clearly. But they did not need to see well. In the darkness of the stable, which reflects the darkness of a world without faith, the sleeping baby is the centre of brightness. Mary is a young girl. We do not see her very clearly, and Joseph is just a background presence. The atmosphere is one of holy awe, one of sheer, grateful wonder. The rough shepherds sink to their knees, peering down at the miraculous baby, who is the Son of God. By not showing us anything outright, Rembrandt makes us search within our own hearts, and imagine what that moment must have been like. It was mysterious. It was holy. It was infinitely comforting and unforgettable. It was a time for prayer, not for talking or trying to reason. It was peace.

23

When Botticelli (1445–1510) painted the birth of Jesus, he wanted to include everything. He sketched a simple stable leading into a cave, and then enclosed the scene with thick, dark tress. It was a sacred spot, set apart for God. His Mary is larger than everyone else, to show that she is greater in spirit than anyone except Jesus. Jesus reaches up to his mother and she adores him, as if they were the only ones present. Joseph is nearly as big as Mary, and he is pondering the mystery of the child. He is sitting behind the baby Jesus, as a safeguard. There, in the sky, are the choirs of angels, dancing and singing and holding lilies. The lily is a symbol of purity, and the angels are purely spirit. They only seem to have bodies, so they can play ring-a-roses in the air. Botticelli makes us believe that his angels are as light as air, and that the great golden sky in the top of the picture is their heavenly home. Three of them, crowned with flowers, have alighted like lovely butterflies on the roof of the stable, and are waving branches and rejoicing. If we look at the ground, there are more angels on the right, leading the shepherds to the crib, and on the left, we see the rich people. All are welcome. One angel is tenderly showing a shepherd that he should push back his hood, for this is a holy place. The angel in pink on the other side is gently encouraging the rich men to come closer, not to be afraid. But then we look lower still, to where the earth opens up into deep cracks and crevices. There we can seen devils vanishing into these crevices. They are furious, for now they cannot stay on earth: Jesus has come, and he has brought love with him. Angels and men are embracing, although angels are pure spirit and human beings are not. We all have bad sides; we all do things that are wrong, even if we are sorry for what we have done afterwards. But since Jesus has been born, the angels can help us better. Notice how one man comes really close to the angel, the next man not so close, and the third holds back slightly. We have to make the effort to receive this strength and angelic goodness, and we can only do this if we chose to. Botticelli has painted a great scene of forgiveness and joy, to show the importance of the birth of Jesus to each and every one of us.

Like Botticelli, Jacob van Oostsanen (1470 – 1533) wants to include everything. He has painted a lovely picture of Mary, with her long golden curls shimmering in the light. He has also included a handsome Joseph, joining Mary in prayer. He is as dark as she is fair. For a carpenter, which was Joseph's job, his hands are very delicate, but maybe they are stronger than they look, since he is otherwise a powerful man — a good protector. The shepherds have answered the angelic summon, and they are very well behaved. They are standing outside, looking in. We can see that there are far more to come, because there are still people in the fields who have just heard the wonderful message and are beginning to move towards the stable. They are coming so quietly that the sheep are not alarmed. We can only hope that they will realize that this building is the stable, because van Oostsanen shows that he is certain that Jesus could not have been born in an ordinary place. His stable is supported by grand pillars with red and white stonework — although he tries to keep his feet on the ground by showing a roof with holes in it and by erecting a wooden arrangement to the right. Furthermore, the angels are busily taking over. There is a whole set of them in the rafters, stringing up Christmas decorations, and angel bands are striking up on every side. There are angels of all sizes: tiny ones for the tiny Jesus, lying sweetly amidst all this commotion, toddler-sized angels behind the crib to serenade the baby more directly, and adult angels to keep Mary and Joseph company. Wherever you look, angels are taking over. There is only one angel actually outside the stable, because the visible world is not one where angels would feel comfortable. Near the fields there are the cottages of the poorer people, but on the peculiar looking rock formation, there seem to be several castles. The people who live in them are out of touch with reality, and what van Oostsanen is saying is that the angelic world is the real world. All this innocence and happiness, this singing and music-making, this delight in life: this is what the birth of Jesus brings us, and that is why we celebrate at Christmas. It is why we give presents, why we have special meals, and why we have fun as a family. The painting may be a little over the top, but the message is clear and true: be happy, Jesus is born this Christmas Day!

27

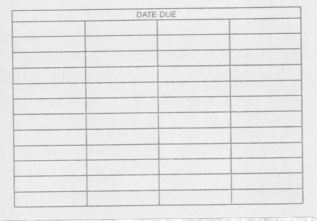

*T*hese details are all
taken from the paintings in this book. Can
you find them and name the artists?

28